Captain Cook

Rebecca Levene

Illustrated by David Cuzik

Historical advice:
John Woolley, Education Officer
Captain Cook Memorial Museum, Whitby

Series editor: Lesley Sims

Designed by Russell Punter

First published in 2005 by Usborne Publishing Ltd.,
Usborne House, 83-85 Saffron Hill, London
EC1N 8RT, England.
www.usborne.com

Printed in Spain. UE.
First published in America in 2005.

Contents

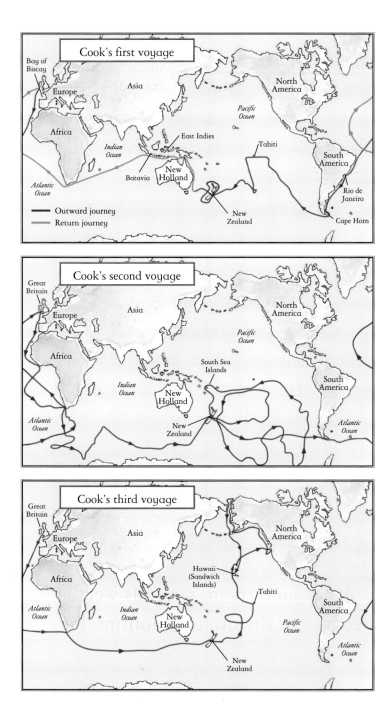

Chapter 1

Off to war

It was a frosty morning and the sun was rising through a haze of white mist as James Cook started work in the fields. He held tight to the reins of a shaggy brown horse as it tilled the earth, churning up dirt. James was only eight, so the horse towered above him, but the animal knew him well and didn't try to pull away.

All around them, seagulls were pecking at the ground, hunting for

worms. They had flown all the
way from the coast to James's
Yorkshire village and at the end of
the day they would fly all the way
back again.

James watched them go, desperately
wishing he could follow. He longed to
be a sailor, to cross the sea and visit
faraway countries – especially
countries no one had ever seen before.

When he was just eighteen, part of
his wish was granted. He was hired as
an apprentice on a boat taking coal

from Whitby, one of Britain's largest ports, to London. The other sailors complained about the back-breaking work and the coal dust that stained their hands and faces black. James was too thrilled with sailing to care.

He became an expert at handling the flat-bottomed coal boats – known as 'cats' – and after six years he was promoted to ship's mate. It was a responsible job, but by now James wasn't so happy. When he'd dreamed of being a sailor, he had imagined exploring exotic new places, not sailing to and from smog-filled London.

Eventually, at the age of twenty-six, he decided to volunteer for the Royal Navy. His shipmates thought he was crazy.

"Don't you know there's a war coming?" one of them asked. "You'll be killed for sure."

"Even if you aren't killed, you'll wish you were dead," another said. "Have you heard how they treat men in the navy? They give you twelve lashes just for speaking out of turn!"

James wasn't put off. "I want to see the world," he told the others, "and joining the navy is the best way to do it. Besides, if there is a war, I want to fight for my country."

He didn't have to wait long. In May 1756, Britain and France declared war. Two years later, the captain of James's ship called his crew together. "I've received new orders," he announced. "We're to sail with the fleet to the American colonies. We're taking the army to fight the French for control of the town of Quebec."

To reach Quebec they had to sail thousands of miles across the Atlantic. It was a terrible journey. Winds tore at the sails and the waves were so high they threatened to crash over the decks and wash everyone into the sea.

Worst of all, many of the sailors were struck down by scurvy, a disease caused by a lack of fresh fruit and vegetables. It left the sailors so exhausted they could hardly move. As the weeks passed, more and more men died.

At last, one morning from high in the rigging, the lookout shouted, "Land ho!" They had reached the tree-lined coast of Canada.

As the ship drew in to shore, James felt a moment's panic. He knew the French army was waiting for them, and would fight hard to hold on to their land.

His fear was quickly replaced by a rising feeling of excitement. He had crossed an ocean and arrived on a new continent. Whatever lay ahead, he was ready.

Chapter 2

Master map-maker

Fierce fighting soon broke out between the British and French armies. Hundreds of soldiers on both sides were killed, as the French defended a large fort at the mouth of the St. Lawrence river. Finally, the British won and the sailors celebrated with rum and song. James was too worried to join in.

"Enjoy yourself while you can," one of his shipmates told him. "We're about to take our soldiers up the river to Quebec itself."

"That's what I'm worried about," James admitted. "I've heard the river is filled with hidden rocks and we only have basic charts. Without a decent chart to guide us, our ships could sink."

Luckily, a lieutenant in the British army, Samuel Holland, had been charting the riverbank near the fort. When James shared his fears, Samuel agreed to teach him how to plot the layout of a riverbed.

Feeling a little happier, James went to see the captain, who was pacing up and down in his cabin.

"I don't see how we'll ever get to Quebec in one piece," he groaned.

"Let me help," said James. "If you can give me some time, I'll draw you a chart of the river all the way from here to Quebec."

James was as good as his word. Despite freezing weather and the constant danger of French attacks, as they sailed up the St. Lawrence river he managed to draw an approximate chart of the riverbed. Thanks to James, the British fleet reached Quebec unscathed.

Three years passed before the war ended and James could return to London. While there on leave, he met and married a young woman named Elizabeth. By the time he left her to return to his ship, she was pregnant with their first child.

Over the next few years, James put his map-making skills to use as he charted the coast of Newfoundland — a part of Canada the British had won from the French. He was happy to be doing something so useful...

...and the more he worked, the greater his skill grew.

Back in London, his officers had been talking about James's amazing talent. For many years, scientists in the Royal Society had been trying to discover how far the Earth was from the Sun. To find out, they needed someone to travel to the other side of the world and measure the position of the planet Venus at the exact moment it passed in front of the Sun. This was known as the Transit of Venus, and it didn't happen very often.

James seemed the perfect choice. He was summoned home to meet the Earl of Sandwich, the man in charge of the entire British navy.

"James," the Earl declared, "I need a talented navigator to measure the Transit of Venus. How would you like to have command of your own ship and sail her to the South Seas?"

"Really?" James could hardly believe it. At last he'd be able to explore places no British person had ever visited.

"But you have to hurry," the Earl went on. "If you don't reach the South Seas in time, there won't be another Transit of Venus for a hundred years."

Chapter 3

The long voyage

James's ship was a small wooden 'cat' named *Endeavour*. Her flat base was perfect for exploring unknown coastlines and James thought her the most beautiful ship he'd ever seen.

Thanks to his occasional visits home on leave, he now had three children to wave him off. Elizabeth, expecting their fourth child, was in tears as they said goodbye.

"Don't worry about me," James

reassured her. "They're sending a troop of soldiers along to keep us safe."

A Royal Astronomer went with him, to supervise the actual measuring, as well as two botanists – Joseph Banks and Daniel Solander – who were going to record all the new plants and animals encountered during the trip.

As the crew loaded the ship with food, including cackling hens, a messenger handed James a sealed envelope.

"These are secret orders from the Admiralty," the man told him. "Only open them when you're safely at sea."

Intrigued, James could hardly wait to break the seal. Inside the envelope he found orders to search for the Great Southern Continent. This mysterious land was supposed to lie in the Pacific, though no one had ever found it. Every country wanted a place they could claim for themselves and then exploit, and imagined it might be like Europe.

The *Endeavour* was barely under way when she was caught in a violent storm in the Bay of Biscay. Waves smashed on to the decks and all the hens were washed overboard.

Undaunted, Cook sailed on. As they crossed the equator, the imaginary line dividing the northern hemisphere from the south, a sailor approached James with a grin on his face.

"Sir," he declared, "it's a tradition that every man crossing the equator for the first time has to be dunked in the sea."

James thought it sounded hideous and offered everyone rum if they'd let him off. His crew, happy with the bribe, agreed.

Having crossed the Atlantic, they landed in Rio de Janeiro in Brazil. James was expecting a friendly welcome, but the Viceroy who ran the city thought James and his men were British spies.

"Who sails thousands of miles to

study a planet?" he scoffed.

When he heard the ship needed to stock up on supplies, he declared James alone could leave the ship to get them. James tried to explain he needed his men to help him and some of the crew were thrown in prison.

In the end, the Viceroy agreed to release them – on condition James left Rio as quickly as possible.

From Brazil the *Endeavour* sailed around Cape Horn and into the Pacific Ocean. Before them lay the beautiful palm-fringed island of Tahiti. Excited Tahitians scrambled into wooden canoes and sailed over to greet James and his men.

"What are they wearing?" sniffed Banks, looking at the Tahitians' simple clothes.

"I hope he isn't rude to them," James thought. "They could hurt us if we upset them." He invited the Tahitian chieftains on board his ship and, as a gesture of friendship, they exchanged gifts.

James produced metal hatchets for the chiefs, who were ecstatic. Metal was non-existent on Tahiti, so it was extremely valuable.

To thank James for his friendship and generosity, the Tahitians agreed to let the Royal Astronomer set up his telescope on their land. On a bright, clear day he measured the Transit of Venus and completed his mission for the Royal Society.

But James knew that the most difficult task still lay ahead of them: the search for the elusive Great Southern Continent.

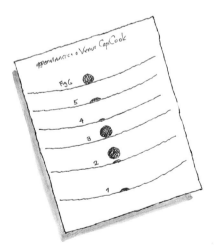

Chapter 4

Uncharted waters

James's men were reluctant to leave Tahiti. Many had fallen in love with local women and asked if they could stay behind.

"You're sailors in the Royal Navy," James told them angrily. "Get back aboard the ship right now!"

Grumbling, the men obeyed.

James headed south, stopping off at dazzling islands along the way, to explore and meet the islanders.

Everywhere they went, Banks kept a note of the unusual creatures they saw. "Look at that!" he said, when he spotted a funny black-and-white bird waddling across a rock. "I can't wait to tell everyone at home about this."

"They probably won't believe you," James commented, with a grin. "Some of these animals are so strange, people will think you're making them up."

As the weeks passed, they found plenty of new and fascinating plants and animals – but they didn't find anything that looked like the Great Southern Continent.

James decided to
change direction and,
soon afterwards, a
lookout spotted a
great mass of land.

"That's it!" Banks
cried in excitement.
"We've found it."

"I'm not so sure,"
James replied, doubtfully. He was right.
Instead of the Great Southern Continent
they had found New Zealand. And a
Dutchman, Abel Tasman, had been
there already, although he hadn't
realized how big it was.

Some of the island's inhabitants, the
Maoris, spotted James's ship. To them,
the *Endeavour* looked like a huge bird,
its white sails flapping in the breeze
like wings. Fearing the sailors on board

had come to conquer the land and kill all their people, the Maoris attacked.

Instantly, the sailors fired into the Maoris' advancing ranks. The Maoris, who had never seen a gun before, were amazed and then appalled when some of their men dropped dead.

"But guns won't stop them forever," thought James. "Besides, we have to avoid more bloodshed." He didn't want to kill the Maoris who, after all, were only protecting their land.

"Hold your fire," James directed his crew sternly. "I want you to take some of their young men hostage, instead."

The sailors did as they were told, expecting James to threaten the hostages to force the other Maoris to behave. They were astonished when James simply gave the young men gifts, then released them again.

"He's asking for trouble!" they muttered, but James knew what he was doing. When the hostages returned to their people, they described how well James had treated them.

The Maoris quickly realized that the strangers didn't mean them any harm and from then on, James and his crew traded with them in peace.

After drawing the first ever complete map of New Zealand – which turned out to consist of two huge islands – James decided it was time to begin the long journey back to England. He and his men had been at sea for nearly two years and they were desperate to see their homes and families again.

Of course, James still hadn't found the Great Southern Continent, but by now he was fairly sure that it didn't exist. Wanting to do as much exploring as possible, he decided to take a different route home, along the coast of a vast country named New Holland (and now known as Australia).

James sailed along the east coast of New Holland, the first European to see it. He drew detailed maps of every stage, naming each place after his crew or important people back in England.

Eventually, they came to an area of sea filled with islands and sandbanks. Suddenly, James heard a loud grating noise and the whole ship juddered. Some of the men shouted in panic. James felt his own heart race. They'd hit disaster – the bottom of the ship had struck a coral reef.

Chapter 5

Disaster!

The *Endeavour* was stuck fast. Worst of all, the coral had torn a large hole in the bottom of the ship and it rapidly began to fill with water.

"Man the pumps!" James shouted to his crew. "Throw everything we don't need overboard."

The sailors rushed to obey, hurling iron ballast, empty caskets, spoiled food and even their guns overboard. It made no difference. As the seconds ticked away, the boat filled up with water... faster and faster.

James knew that if they stayed on the reef, the ship would eventually be ground to pieces and they would all die. But, if he did manage to get the *Endeavour* away from the rocks, the water would rush into the hole even more quickly. They could sink before they reached the distant shore.

"What can we do?" the men begged.

James hesitated, knowing that the wrong decision would doom them all. Then he cried, "Every man into the boats! We must pull the ship away from the rocks."

At first, the ship refused to budge. Finally, with another horrendous grating sound, the boats managed to drag the ship away from the coral. But as James had feared, the water began flooding in faster than the men could pump it out.

To make things worse, James was finding it almost impossible to navigate a safe way through all the sandbanks to the shore.

He was beginning to despair when Monkhouse, a young midshipman, rushed up to him. "Sir," he said breathlessly, "What about 'fothering'? I've done it before."

"Of course!" cried James.

'Fothering' meant holding a spare sail under the bottom of the ship to plug the hole. It was certainly worth a try.

For a moment, it looked as if the sail wouldn't be strong enough. Then a shout went up. "It's worked!" cried a sailor. "The water's stopped coming in."

The entire crew gave a huge cheer. Thanks to James and Midshipman Monkhouse, they were able to reach the shore safely, although they had to spend several weeks repairing the ship.

With the *Endeavour* fixed, James headed for the East Indies. The area had been taken over by the Dutch and James was confident he and his men would be safe. He couldn't have been more wrong.

When they pulled into port at the capital, Batavia, they saw the white, drawn faces of very sick men lining the shore. The whole city was riddled with dysentery and malaria.

James left Batavia as soon as he could but it was too late. Most of his sailors were already infected. By the time he made it back to England, 41 of them had died.

The remaining crew returned to London as heroes. Banks and Solander became celebrities and hogged the limelight so much that the expedition became known as the Banks-Solander voyage. But the Earl of Sandwich was delighted with James and made him a commander. From now on, he would be addressed as Captain James Cook.

James was thrilled, though his happiness was shattered with some dreadful news. While he was away at sea, both his daughter and youngest son had died. Over the next few months, James spent a lot of time mourning his children and all the men who had lost their lives on his voyage. He knew he had achieved great things – but they had been at a high price.

Chapter 6

Hidden danger

Although James insisted that the so-called Great Southern Continent didn't exist, the staff at the Admiralty weren't convinced and ordered him back to the Pacific to search again. This time, he would have two small ships at his command: the *Resolution* and the *Adventure*.

Botanist Joseph Banks was supposed to go along too. Unfortunately, his new-found fame had gone to his head, making him act like a rock star.

"I'd be delighted to accompany James," Banks told the Earl of Sandwich, "but the ship was very cramped last time. I'll need an extra deck for my luggage and servants."

"That's a terrible idea," James argued. "Another deck will be too heavy. The ship will capsize."

James was ignored and, sure enough, when the newly refitted ship set sail, it nearly sank. The exhausted carpenters, who'd spent so much time adding the extra deck, had to spend months taking it out again. Banks was furious and refused to sail. James pretended to be disappointed but was really relieved to be rid of the rather demanding young man.

At last, James set sail again. The further south he voyaged, the colder it became, until his two ships found themselves sailing past enormous icebergs. The tops of the icebergs towered above them, but most of the ice was hidden below the water's surface. Any ship could sail into an iceberg without realizing it was there and be destroyed.

The cold became almost unbearable. The sailors put on their warmest clothes but still complained they couldn't feel their fingers or toes. Then the water supply began to run dangerously low.

James tried not to show it, but he was worried. Even if they turned back now, they'd probably die of thirst before they reached land. And then he had an idea. "Bring some ice from the

icebergs," he ordered.

The sailors were puzzled. "He's crazy," the men muttered to each other. "The icebergs are frozen sea water. They'll be far too salty to drink." But the sailors were wrong. The melted ice made perfect drinking water.

That problem was no sooner solved than they hit another one. The icebergs were too close together to sail between.

James had to accept defeat. Turning around, they set off to explore the South Sea islands instead. Things were going well until a great storm blew up, separating the two ships.

The navigator aboard the *Resolution* was in despair. "We'll never find the *Adventure* now," he said to James.

"Don't worry," James reassured him. "The captain and I already agreed that, if this ever happened, we'd meet up in New Zealand."

Fighting their way through the storm, they headed to New Zealand to wait. After several days, with no sign of the other crew, some of James's sailors began to suggest they'd been killed. The sailors had been panicked by the Maoris' ancient custom of eating the bodies of men killed in battle. James calmed down his crew and took them off exploring again.

When the *Adventure* finally arrived, four days later, her captain decided to return home. Then, the day before they sailed for England, ten of the crew were killed in a fight with some Maoris.

Meanwhile, James was continuing with his mission, heading further south than any person had sailed before. At last, he found a vast sheet of ice spreading across the horizon, glittering white in the brilliant sunshine.

For all James knew it stretched to the South Pole and – even if he had realized there could be land underneath – it wasn't what he was looking for. He had sailed all over the Pacific Ocean, but he could go no further.

Chapter 7

Third time unlucky

When James arrived home, his wife was delighted, especially as he was promoted, with the official title post-captain, and given a land-based job in Greenwich. Finally, they could be together for more than a few weeks.

The Admiralty accepted that the Great Southern Continent didn't exist. This just made ministers eager to find something people had sought for two hundred years: the Northwest Passage, a sea route linking the Atlantic and the Pacific across the top of Canada.

The Earl of Sandwich asked James who should lead the expedition to find it. But every time he suggested a name, James rejected it.

"This is stupid," James said, at last. "Only one captain can complete the mission – me."

"We can't ask you to leave your family again," protested the Earl.

"My country comes first," James replied.

The truth was, although he loved his family, he loved adventuring more.

Both his ships needed a lot of work before they could sail. Unfortunately, James was sick in the months leading up to the journey. Without him to keep an eye on things, the shipyards did a shoddy job. The carpenters sat around when they should have been working and nobody checked that everything was put together properly.

Lots of countries were looking for the Northwest Passage and the Admiralty wanted to keep James's mission secret. So they pretended James was simply revisiting Tahiti. Then George III asked James to take a bull and cows along, plus sheep, horses and even peacocks.

"I want the people of Tahiti to learn how to farm the English way," he said.

James didn't think the Tahitians needed much help with their farming. But he was only a captain in the navy, even if he was a famous one, and had to do what his King told him.

As soon as both ships set sail, the problems started. Because of the animals, the ships were smelly and crowded. Then the *Resolution* sprang a leak, ruining all the sails that were kept in the store room. Not wanting to lose too much time, James gave the order to keep going.

On the way, they stopped at a group of islands no European had ever seen. James named them the Sandwich Islands, after the Earl, but he sailed on after only two weeks. He needed to head north before winter set in.

Already, the weather was worsening. Storms raged and freezing rain seeped through their clothes until it felt as if their bones were made of ice. All the way up the west coast of Canada, James looked for the Northwest Passage and found nothing.

One day, he saw they were approaching a huge inlet in the coastline. For the first time in several weeks, he felt some hope.

"It's only a river," his navigator, Bligh, told him. "It's not big enough to go all the way from here to the Atlantic Ocean."

To James's disappointment, Bligh was proved right. Soon, they had to turn around and head back north. For weeks, they kept on sailing through the bitter cold, until James saw a sheet of ice almost 4m (12ft) high. It covered the ocean as far as the eye could see.

Only then did he admit defeat. He had searched every inch of the coast, but found no sign of the Northwest Passage. Now there was nothing to do but begin the long, hard journey home.

Chapter 8

Cook's last stand

On the way back, James decided to stop at the Sandwich Islands. First, he sailed all the way around the largest – known to the inhabitants as Hawaii – and drew a map of the coastline, before deciding to explore the island itself.

As his ships neared shore, the largest fleet of canoes James had ever seen came out to greet them, packed with Hawaiian men and women.

He invited some on board, hoping to trade with them. But as soon as they saw him many dropped to their knees crying, "Erono!"

James was baffled. He had no idea that Erono was the Hawaiian God of Peace. According to legend, Erono was supposed to appear in a huge canoe and sail all the way around the island before pulling into the exact bay where James had landed. Completely by accident, James had fulfilled the prophecy – and now the local people thought he was their god.

Immediately, one of the most important chiefs on the island came to meet James and, almost everywhere they went, he and his men were showered with gifts. Some of the local tribes were less friendly. They doubted that James really was Erono. Besides, even if he was, Erono's time of year was nearly over. It would soon be the season of the God of War.

At last, James left. But as his ships headed out to sea, a terrifying storm blew up. With an ominous crack, the foremast of the *Resolution* split.

"What shall we do?" Bligh asked James. "I'm not sure we'll be welcome back on Hawaii."

"Well, we can't keep sailing," James replied. "We'll lose the mast before we reach the next island."

Reluctantly, he gave the order to return to Hawaii. It was a bad move. As Bligh had guessed, the Hawaiians weren't pleased to see them. The sailors were pelted with stones and some members of one of the more unfriendly tribes sneaked on board the *Resolution* and stole a rowing boat.

Hoping to prevent a major battle, James took the important Hawaiian chief hostage. He led him to the ships, surrounded by his men and a group of furious Hawaiians.

"Be careful, Captain," one of his soldiers said. "They look angry."

"Don't worry, they won't do anything," James replied confidently. "Just keep moving."

But before James could reach the water, news reached the Hawaiians that another of their chiefs had been

killed by James's men. The Hawaiians
were incensed. Some of them picked
up lumps of rock and threw them at
the sailors.

"Fire your guns!" James ordered,
hoping to scare the Hawaiians away.

That just made the Hawaiians even
angrier. Lifting their clubs, they raced
over and the sailors panicked. Without
waiting for James, they turned and ran.

James was left unprotected, but for a moment the Hawaiians hung back, afraid to hurt him in case he really was the god Erono. Then one of them crept up and hit James with a club. When James fell to his knees, the other Hawaiians knew he was only human like them. They rushed forward and attacked.

On the shore of Hawaii, a few steps away from safety, Captain James Cook died.

He had explored more of the world than any other person before him, but his greatest achievement was to draw incredibly accurate maps of his travels – and then make them public.

During James's lifetime, people rushed to read about his voyages. And, almost two centuries after his death, his maps were still being used by sailors, explorers and adventurers.

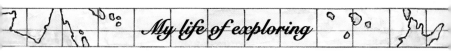

1728 - I am born in Marton in Yorkshire.

1746 - I get my first job as a sailor, transporting coals from Whitby to London.

1755 - War with France is approaching and I volunteer for the Royal Navy.

1759 - My maps of the St. Lawrence river help the British to reach and thus capture Quebec.

*1768 - My first big adventure begins as I head off to the Pacific in the **Endeavour** for the Transit of Venus.*

1770 - Our ship hits a coral reef. Luckily, the quick-thinking Midshipman Monkhouse saves the day.

1771 - I get a promotion. From now on I'll be Captain Cook.

*1772 - I set off on my second voyage. This time, I'm allowed to take two ships, the **Resolution** and the **Adventure**.*

1773 - We're surrounded by huge icebergs. Sailing through them, I go as far south as anyone's ever been.

1775 - I return home, to promotion and a job in Greenwich.

1776 - I set off on my third voyage. This time I'm looking for the Northwest Passage.

1778 - I visit Hawaii briefly, before sailing as close to the North Pole as it's possible to go. There's no sign of the Northwest Passage.

1779 - I return to Hawaii, where some of the locals think I'm a god. But then I'm forced to return a third time, when they're less friendly.

On February 14th, 1779, James Cook was killed by angry Hawaiians.